MISSION: PARENTING

Dad's Survival Guide to the Toddler Years

Creative, Graphic Design & Illustrations: Yael Eshet
Thoughts & Comments: Rachel Stein
Graphic Execution: Liron Avrami
Editor: Estee Lavitt
ISBN 9789655752663

CONTENTS

Note to Self: Most Things That Will Happen.... 008

Being a Dad Is 010

Things You Wish Someone Told You Before You Had A Baby 012

Babies: The Rules 014

The Statistics! 016

Your Life, Then and Now 018

Note to Self: Never tell your wife 020

Questions Dads Ask 022

Vacation With the Kids 024

Moments of Terror! 026

The Statistics! 028

Evolution of Parenting 030

Note to Self: Even if You Played with Your Baby 032

Facts of Life 034

Somebody Needs to Invent 036

The 10 Commandments of 3 Year Olds: Just When Daddy 038

The Statistics! 040

Your Life, Then and Now 042

Note to Self: Everyone knows how to raise kids... 044

When You're Alone With the Kids, and Your Partner Isn't Home 046

Tips That Always Work! 048

The Best In The World 050

The Statistics 052

Note To Self: Bribery 054

The 10 Commandments of 3 Year Olds: Kids - The Rules! 056

Facts of Life: Facts Don't Lie

10 Easy Ways to Wake a Baby

The Statistics!

Your Life, Then and Now

Note to Self: If You're Doing Something Around the House

10 Things That Must be Included in Dad Basic Training

You And Your Partner

10 Things That Dads Do

The Statistics!

Evolution of Parenting

Note to Self: You Don't Achieve Quiet

Dads Ask

The 10 Commandments of 3 Year Olds: Reasons for Hysterics

Things You Wish Someone Told You Before You Had A Baby

The Statistics!

Note To Self: Don't Give Your Kids Names

Things You Didn't Think You Would Do as a Dad

Evolution of Parenting

10 Signs You've Turned into Your Father

The Statistics!

Note to Self: You Realize Just How Little You Know

058

060

062

064

066

068

070

072

074

076

078

080

082

084

086

088

090

092

094

096

098

Note
to
Self

Most things that will
happen to you as a dad
**cannot be found
in any guide book.**

Being a Dad

IS

1 Finding pieces of half-eaten pancake in your pants pocket.

2 Arriving at an interview on a rainy day with a small, pink umbrella because that's what you had in the car.

3 Playing with your baby for three hours only to realize it's been just 20 minutes.

4 Having the boss over for dinner and finding that the only ice cubes left are shaped like airplanes.

5 Buying a new playstation as a gift "for the kid."

6 Being excited when the baby calls you "Dada," and then realizing that the plant, the cat and the TV are also "Dada."

7 Never eating the food you love, but whatever's left in the fridge and is about to go bad.

8 Explaining to your child that candy isn't healthy, and then eating an entire chocolate bar by yourself after she goes to sleep.

9 Pretending to film the kindergarten party, while secretly watching ESPN on your phone.

10 Very quietly opening the closet door in the kids' room at bedtime, just to make sure there really aren't any monsters there.

*Things You Wish
Someone Told You*

BEFORE YOU
HAD A BABY

1. A baby is actually an alarm clock that you can't turn off.

2. Feeding a one-year-old baby is like turning on a blender and forgetting the lid.

3. Trying to put a screaming baby into the car seat is like trying to fit a wet octopus into a small plastic bag.

4. Birth is the beginning of the longest babysitting shift ever.

5. A dad's brain looks like cauliflower that's been smashed to a pulp.

6. The baby will always wake up sick the morning you have an important presentation at work.

7. "Summer vacation" isn't really a vacation.

8. The volume button on kids' toys doesn't actually work.

9. You'll love your kids more than anything on this earth, but mostly when they're sleeping.

10. Kids don't come with an exchange policy and there's no customer service.

Babies:

THE RULES

1. The smaller the baby, the more room he takes up in his parents' bed.

2. Every baby has more clothing than both of his parents - combined.

3. It doesn't matter how many toys the baby has, he'll only want to play with the TV remote control.

4. If baby smiles at you when you've just changed her diaper, it's not a smile, she's pooping.

5. If you put your baby in a onesie, there will always be one more snap left.

6. If your wife isn't home and you're dressing the baby by yourself - you'll never find two matching socks.

7. The more expensive the shirt you're wearing, the greater the odds that baby will spit up on you.

8. All of the good pacifiers always disappear once the cleaning lady goes home.

9. There are no bad children. There are children who didn't go down for their naps.

10. Don't believe whoever tells you that sleepless nights stop at the age of three months. After gas comes teething, and then they start being afraid of monsters.

- the -

STATISTICS!

 **90%** of being a dad is trying not to miss the toilet through the potty-training seat while sporting morning wood.

 **90%** of being a dad is having friends over and serving them coffee in Minnie Mouse sippy cups.

 **90%** of the time you imagine the answer to, "Are you full?" comes from the floor saying, "Yes, thank you."

 **90%** of a dad's life is condensed into 10 minutes in the bathroom before the kids wake up.

 **100%** of being a dad is saying, "Good for you, buddy!!" when someone burps at the office.

YOUR LIFE, THEN & NOW

Before
you had a baby

After
you had a baby

Go to bed at 5am.

Get up at 5am.

Go camping for a week with one small backpack.

Go to the park for an hour with two bags, food, toys, and a blanket.

Barely wake up from your alarm.

Who needs an alarm when you have a baby?

Note
to
Self

Never tell your wife,
"I understand what contractions feel like.
Somebody kneed me in the nuts one time."

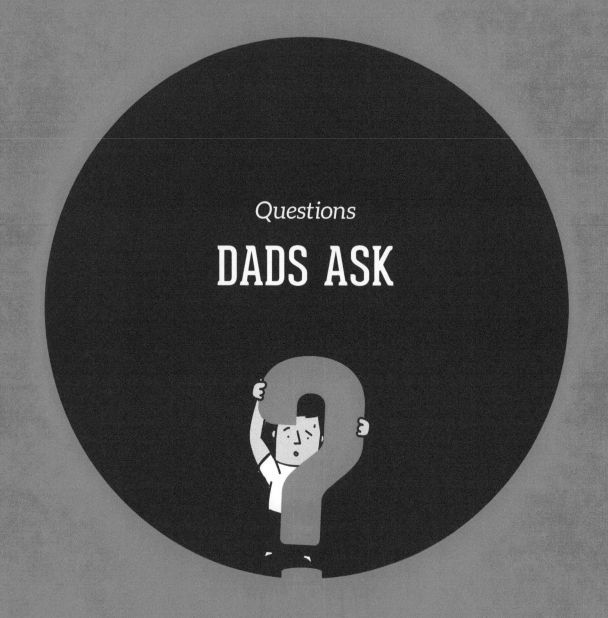

Questions

DADS ASK

1. I looked away for a second and the baby opened the fridge and smeared garlic butter on herself. Should I wash her? Or just let the dog deal with it?

2. It's the middle of the night, the baby's sleeping, but he has poop in his diaper. Do I have to change him right now? Or can I leave it for my partner? Because her shift starts in 15 minutes.

3. The kid asked me, "Daddy, what is this?" and I have no idea. Can I make it up?

4. My wife's not home and I'm dressing the baby. He won't stop crying. Is it because he needs to be changed? Or is it the colors of the outfit that I chose?

5. Is it physically possible to pick up a baby with a plunger?

6. My son climbed all the way up to the top of the slide, but now he's crying and can't get down. Can I take a selfie with him before I help him down?

7. How common is it to share custody with grandparents? Asking for a friend.

8. Do parents usually ask their kids' friends to sign a non-disclosure agreement?

9. At what point during the pregnancy should I start convincing my partner to name the baby "Wolverine?"

10. My baby was born today. Should I abandon all of my parental principles right now, or can I wait a few days?

Vacation
WITH
THE KIDS

1. "Vacation with kids" isn't really vacation.

2. Your wife wants to take the kids on vacation just so she can post pics and get more "likes."

3. If you disregard the fights, crying, sweat, stress, bugs, boredom, whining, heat or cold, discomfort or lack of sleep - camping is a great vacation idea!

4. There are two types of people at a hotel: those who have fun, and parents with children.

5. 90% of your time at the pool is spent blowing up floaties for the kids.

6. 90% of your time at the pool is spent taking your kids to the bathroom.

7. Your little girl will always need to pee while you're standing in the longest line for the water slide.

8. Despite your partner's protests, throwing coins into the pool is in fact a legit way to teach your son to swim.

9. No matter where you go to sleep, there will always be a band of crickets outside the window.

10. After the kids go to bed: Your partner - straightens the clothes, prepares the bags for tomorrow. You - calculate just how much the vacation has cost you so far.

Moments of

TERROR!

1. When you have a sleeping baby in your arms and you feel a sneeze coming on.

2. When your daughter asks you how kids come from Daddy's penis.

3. When you're alone with your daughter and her preschool friend and the friend says, "Jane's Daddy, I need to go poo."

4. When your wife tries to put the baby to sleep and you accidentally flush the toilet.

5. When you realize that you forgot to pick up your son from preschool, even though your wife reminded you twice.

6. When another dad brings his son over for a playdate and, instead of leaving, he says, "I think I'll stay a while."

7. When you realize at 5pm that one of your kids is napping too close to bedtime.

8. When you're spending the day outdoors with your child and realize you forgot to bring his blankie.

9. When you wake up in the middle of the night and see your child staring at you.

10. When you tiptoe into the kids' room while they're sleeping and one of them starts to move.

- the -
STATISTICS!

 of being a dad is sorting through puzzle pieces.

 of being a dad is hearing how preschool went today.

 of being a dad is picking out the vegetable pieces out of the kids' food.

 of being a dad is taking a photo of your kids eating something healthy when they're with you so your wife will see the effort you put in.

 of the time at the end of a meal there will be cereal scattered on the floor. Even if the kids didn't eat cereal.

EVOLUTION
of
PARENTING

New Dad

VS

Veteran Dad

New Dad	VS	Veteran Dad
Takes the temperature of the water with a special thermometer.	Bath	Dips a finger in and says, "that seems right."
Everything new, designer label.	Clothes	The baby boy wears his big sister's skirts.
Makes sure the story is educational enough.	Bedtime Story	Makes sure the story is short enough.

Note
to
Self

Even if you played with your baby
for four hours straight -
**your partner will come in exactly when you check
something on your phone.**

1. A baby that falls asleep on you will weigh exactly twice his actual weight.

2. The ice cream truck will always have only one popsicle in the flavor that both kids want.

3. If you move the couch at any given moment, you'll find a pacifier and a half eaten cookie.

4. When the kids scratch their heads, it's not because they're thinking hard. They just have lice.

5. The stage in which baby wakes up on time, doesn't cry in the middle of the night, and goes to bed early lasts for exactly two days.

6. If the baby falls asleep in the car on the way home from daycare, he won't fall asleep again until tomorrow.

7. There's nothing that makes a new dad happy quite as much as his baby farting.

8. When you're sitting next to a screaming baby at a restaurant, they won't let you change tables if that baby is yours.

9. Your single friends aren't really happy to talk to your son on the phone. So stop it!

10. When your child asks you to play, she really means for you to sit and watch without touching anything.

Somebody

NEEDS TO INVENT

1. A pacifier with a volume button.

2. A timer to set babies back an hour when daylight savings ends.

3. An app that randomly yells out: "Be careful!!" "Don't touch that!!" and "How many times do I have to tell you??"

4. A social media platform to sublet kids.

5. A crying corner for parents at the playground.

6. Vodka candy for dads during summer break.

7. An app that creates photos of you and your child at the playground and automatically sends it to your partner, while you're both actually at home watching ESPN.

8. A child-wash for kids who come home after baseball practice.

9. Legos that become soft when you step on them.

10. An app that alerts you when your son has actually reached the important part of his story.

The 10 Commandments of 3 Year Olds

JUST WHEN DADDY HAS TO LEAVE THE HOUSE...

1. Remember you need to poop.

2. Throw up on your clothes.

3. Spill chocolate milk on yourself.

4. Or glue.

5. Remember that you have to finish putting your entire train set together. .

6. Or take it apart.

7. Lose the **good** pacifier.

8. Try to fit all of your toys in your underwear.

9. Insist on eating every single cornflake s-e-p-a-r-a-t-e-l-y.

10. Insist on wearing all of your costumes, one on top of the other.

- the -
STATISTICS!

 **90%** of being a dad is waiting for your kids to fall asleep.

 **90%** of being a dad is telling Dad Jokes.

 **50%** of being a dad is pretending you know how to fix things so you can impress the kids.

 **50%** of being a dad is breaking down and calling a professional.

 **99%** of your private life as a dad is condensed into an hour and a half at night that begins when the baby falls asleep and ends with you crashing on the couch.

YOUR LIFE,
THEN & NOW

Before
you had a baby

After
you had a baby

Sleep for 12 hours straight.

You need three nights of sleep to make it to 12 hours.

Sex:
Shhh, you'll wake the neighbors!!!

Sex:
Shhh, you'll wake the baby!!!

When you need a break from life: you go surfing.

When you need a break from life: you schedule a long appointment at the dentist.

Note
to
Self

Everyone knows how to raise kids.
Except people who have kids.

When You're Alone
With the Kids, and

YOUR PARTNER
ISN'T HOME

1   Burgers for breakfast!

2   Dry their clothes in the microwave!

3   Tell them to hide and count to a million, then go to sleep.

4   Take them to grandma's house.

5   Clean the entire house with one wet-wipe.

6   Teach the kids how to fight.

7   Encourage the kids to wrestle with each other so they'll get tired and fall asleep early.

8   Put the kids in a box in the living room so they won't make the house dirty.

9   Check to see if a few drops of whisky on a pacifier actually help baby fall asleep.

10   Throw your rules away and let the kids watch another episode on TV.

Tips That
ALWAYS
WORK!

1. If you want to make the kid eat something - put it on your plate.

2. If you want to make the kid want something - give it to another kid.

3. If you want your child to come the first time you call him - yell: "I've called you five times already, how many times do I have to tell you???"

4. If your child says he's bored - tell him to clean the living room.

5. If you want to teach the child math - give him and his siblings unequal allowances.

6. If you can't wake your daughter up in the morning - whisper in her ear that it's Sunday. She'll be up immediately.

7. If you want your child to clean his room - hide money in there and tell him to look for it.

8. If you want to get rid of the drawings your son brought home from preschool - put them in an album and give it to his teacher at the end of the year as a gift.

9. If you're feeding a baby who's less than two years old - throw the food straight on the floor to save time.

10. If you want to drink your coffee hot - go to work.

The Best

IN THE
WORLD

1.

The fastest in the world
A dad who's driving home while his baby is screaming in the back seat.

2.

The happiest in the world
A dad who hears a baby crying and realizes it's not his baby.

3.

The quietest in the world
Parents who are arguing immediately after baby finally falls asleep.

4.

The slowest in the world
A child who's trying to put his socks on while watching TV.

5.
The most embarrassed in the world
A dad whose son calls him from the front door, "Daddy, someone from work is here! Are you done pooping yet?"

6.
The stealthiest in the world
A child who should be in bed but is waiting to be told to go.

7.
The strongest in the world
A dad whose baby fell asleep in his arms. An hour ago.

8.
The most satisfied in the world
A dad whose child says goodbye nicely, while other kids depart in tears.

9.
The most stressed in the world
A dad whose baby is sick. And his wife took the baby to the doctor. And the doctor's office is in the mall.

10.
The most pretentious in the world
A dad who succeeds in putting the baby to sleep after his partner tried and failed for two hours.

- the -
STATISTICS!

 **90%** of being a dad is suppressing the urge to tell your wife "I told you so!!!"

 **90%** of being a dad is communicating with your wife using pantomime after the kids fall asleep.

 **50%** of being a dad is worrying because the kids are fighting.

 **50%** of being a dad is worrying because the kids are quiet.

 **90%** of the times you try to put the baby down to sleep, the baby will put you down to sleep instead.

Note
to
Self

Bribery **is so** a method.

The 10 Commandments of 3 Year Olds

KIDS: THE RULES!

1. Wait until Daddy throws away all of the drawings you brought home from daycare and **only then** complain that you can't find the one with the squirrel.

2. If you have a leading role in the play: say you have to poop right when the show starts.

3. If Daddy asks, "What do you want Mommy to have in her tummy?" say, "A doggy!"

4. Cry for half an hour that you don't want to take a bath, and then cry for half an hour that you don't want to get out of the bath.

5. If you're showing Daddy something, place it really close to his face, right in his eyeball.

6. Always insist that you want to wear the clothes that are in the hamper.

7. Always want to eat the thing that just ran out.

8. You must try the public bathrooms **everywhere** you go.

9. If there's a puddle - you must jump in it.

10. You **don't** need a reason to bite.

Facts of Life

FACTS DON'T LIE

1. If two kids are nice to each other - they must have broken something.

2. Even if you don't sleep for a week straight, you still won't be able to finish everything you need to do.

3. When you tell your child something and say, "But don't tell Mommy" - he will tell Mommy. Immediately.

4. When your partner says you're responsible for picking up your child from daycare, she means you're also responsible to remember to do it.

5. Even if you come back from five years in captivity, your child's first question will be, "Daddy, what did you get me??"

6. Sometimes "happiness" is just sitting in the car and listening to the quiet.

7. The moment you say, "Good night," your child will remember to ask you about the meaning of life.

8. There isn't a moment more ridiculous than yelling at your child to stop yelling.

9. When the kids are sleeping you can watch them for hours and burst at the seams with love for them - but that feeling goes away as soon as they wake up.

10. Remember: if a friend invites you to his child's birthday party on Sunday at 9am, he isn't really a friend!

10 Easy Ways

TO WAKE
A BABY

1   Make yourself some food.

2   Get into the shower.

3   Stretch out on the recliner and open a bottle of beer.

4   Think to yourself that the house is too quiet and/or too clean.

5   Start watching the game on TV.

6   Sit on the couch and close your eyes.

7   Get it on with your wife.

8   Think about going out for a cigarette.

9   Tiptoe past the baby's room.

10 Breathe.

- the -
STATISTICS!

 **90%** of being a dad is removing phantom splinters from your kids' feet.

 **90%** of being a dad is looking at the kids who are yelling at you to "Look at this!"

 **90%** of being a dad is trying to remember where you hid the snacks after the kids fall asleep.

 **50%** of the times you give kids good advice they'll ignore it.

 **50%** of the time they'll do the exact opposite.

YOUR LIFE, THEN & NOW

Before
you had a baby

Fantasy:
Rob a Brink's truck.

Living on the edge: going shark diving in Mexico, smoking a joint in the bar bathroom, skydiving.

Seeing a man eating alone makes you sad.

After
you had a baby

Fantasy:
Rob a Huggies truck.

Living on the edge: putting the baby in front of the TV and going for a smoke on the balcony when your partner's about to get home.

Seeing a man eating alone makes you jealous.

Note
to
Self

If you're doing something around the house, make sure your partner knows it. **If she doesn't, it doesn't count.**

10 Things That
Must be Included in

DAD BASIC TRAINING

1. Changing the baby's diaper while he's sleeping.

2. Dressing a three-year-old girl in less than 10 minutes.

3. Searching for the baby's favorite pacifier while he's screaming that he wants it.

4. Catching the baby's food before it hits the wall.

5. Rocking the stroller with your foot for two hours straight.

6. Successfully taking the princess dress off the three-year-old.

7. Putting sunscreen on a four-year-old's face.

8. Walking into a room with sleeping kids while carrying plastic bags.

9. Taking kids to an amusement park on the weekend.

10. Waiting for your three-year-old to open the door with the key by herself, while you're dying to pee.

You

AND YOUR PARTNER

1.   The road to a happy relationship begins with the words, "Honey, you've lost weight!"

2.   Your wife will always be twice as tired as you.

3.   In 90% of your fights, your wife will remember things that haven't happened yet.

4.   When you take a nap in the middle of the day and your partner asks if you slept well, she doesn't really care. She just wants to remind you that you had a nap and she didn't.

5.   You'll know your partner is mad at you when you realize that your shirts are still in the bottom of the hamper.

6.   A mom's role at preschool: decoration committee, holiday committee, teacher's gift coordinator.

7.   A dad's role at preschool: know how to get there.

8.   If your child falls and hurts himself while playing under your supervision - your only concern is that your wife shouldn't notice when you get home.

9.   If your partner tells you she can live without you - immediately tighten all of the jars in the house.

10.   The real role of dads is to support, love, and run to the supermarket five minutes before it closes.

10 Things

THAT
DADS DO

1. Give a presentation at work sporting glitter nail polish.

2. Secretly destroy the toys with the annoying music.

3. Yell, "I love you!" when the child goes back to preschool after summer break, but actually direct it at the teacher.

4. Attempt to open the house door with the car keys due to exhaustion.

5. Develop a diet of pizza crust and chewed pieces of pear.

6. Don't interfere when the kids are fighting because at least they're occupying themselves.

7. Come home after vacationing with the kids and go to work to relax.

8. Tell their friends how much parenting has matured them, then immediately put a pineapple ring on the child's head and take a picture.

9. Find a TV show the baby likes and let her watch it on a loop until she goes to college.

10. Watch a plane take off while alone, and be sad his kid isn't there with him to see it.

- the -
STATISTICS!

 **90%** of being a dad is eating the kids' leftovers.

 **90%** of being a dad is using the child as an excuse to miss social gatherings.

 **90%** of getting ready in the morning is tying the kids' shoelaces.

 **50%** of being a dad is trying to get the kids to fall asleep.

 **50%** of being a dad is trying to wake them up.

EVOLUTION

of

PARENTING

New Dad	VS	Veteran Dad
A dedicated photo album.	Photos	Cellphone pictures.
Say, "Da-da, Da-da!"	The baby starts talking	Say, "Ma-ma" and only call her, not me!
Makes sure there are good counselors and first aid kits.	The child goes away to camp	Makes sure the child doesn't come home before the end of August.

Note
to
Self

You don't achieve quiet.
You buy it.

DADS ASK

1. What's the difference between pantyhose and tights?

2. What's the difference between a skirt and a dress?

3. It's 5:30pm and the baby looks like she's getting tired. Can I give her some coffee so she won't fall asleep too early and ruin my night?

4. The baby peed in the bath as soon as I put him in. Can I leave him in there or do I have to change the water?

5. Baby pooped on the way to preschool. Can I give him to the teacher like that, or do I have to stop and change his diaper?

6. My daughter wants to eat something yummy from my plate. Is it cool to tell her it's really spicy so she won't want it?

7. Is playing "The Quiet Game" with the child considered spending quality time?

8. Is letting the kid brush the dog's teeth considered quality time with the dog?

9. Is running through the sprinklers at the park considered the bath before bed?

10. The first child was home with my wife for three years. The second, for two. Is it cool to ask her to give birth to the third at daycare?

The 10 Commandments of 3 Year Olds

REASONS FOR HYSTERICS

1. Your pasta touched the ketchup.

2. There's a leaf of parsley on your meatball.

3. You're being asked to wear socks.

4. Daddy didn't let you go into the bathroom with him.

5. Your band-aid got wet in the bath.

6. You can't get your hand out of the sleeve!

7. There's a giraffe on TV!!! And you really don't!!! want to see a giraffe!!! on TV!!!

8. There are peas!!! In the pea soup!!!

9. You wanted to do it by yourself!!! And Daddy helped you anyway!!!

10. You ate a marker and now your mouth is purple.

*Things You Wish
Someone Told You*

BEFORE YOU
HAD A BABY

1. That the longest stretch of parenting is from birth to college.

2. That the only party you'll go to as a dad is the PTA mixer.

3. That whenever you blow up the inflatable mattress at the pool, you'll always end up intimately embracing it.

4. That nothing prepares you for the moment the hippie mom from preschool sends recipes that call for breastmilk.

5. That the minute you come back from vacation the kids will complain that they're bored.

6. That running after twins at the playground is harder than running a marathon.

7. That picking up a sleeping child from a carseat is harder than lifting weights.

8. That you'll always feel the need to announce being a dad when taking your baby girl to a public restroom so people won't be suspicious.

9. That your kid got the good genes from your side of the family. The bad genes are obviously from the other side.

10. That although you always wanted to be a good dad, it's really hard when you actually have kids.

- the -
STATISTICS!

 of being a dad is playing dollhouse for 17 hours without a break.

 of being a dad is saying goodbye to sleeping in.

 of being a dad is wanting your child to be your friend.

 of being a dad is being sad when you drop baby at preschool and he cries when you leave.

 of being a dad is being sad when you drop baby at preschool and he doesn't cry when you leave.

Note
to
Self

Don't give your kids names
that are too exotic.
**The world isn't ready for
a MLB pitcher named "Mango."**

*Things You Didn't Think
You Would Do*

AS
A DAD

1. Speak of yourself in third person ("Daddy's mad!! Daddy doesn't let you draw on the wall!!!").

2. Hide in the bathroom while eating your son's last candy bar.

3. Say "Amazing!!" when you see two milk cartons that were glued together with glitter.

4. Watch the same animated movie eight times a day. For three months straight.

5. Explain to the boss that you were late for the meeting because your daughter couldn't decide if she wanted to drink her chocolate milk from the blue cup or the orange cup.

6. Find yourself saying "no!" in the snack aisle at the supermarket even though you're alone.

7. Pick up all the Legos while simultaneously yelling at your child that you "won't pick up the Legos for him!!!"

8. Warn your daughter not to spill that!!! as she spills whatever it is all over the place.

9. Try to calm a child who's screaming because you wouldn't get her a REAL zebra.

10. Turn on the TV after the baby finally falls asleep only to stare at the baby channel for two hours.

EVOLUTION
of
PARENTING

New Dad	VS	Veteran Dad
Uses boiled water in a sterile bottle.	The baby is thirsty	Lets him drink from the hose in the backyard.
Educational books, board games, removes the TV from the house.	Passing the time	Cellphone for every child, TV in every room, buys the baby a tablet as a present at birth.
Special safety car seat, double seatbelt, head guard.	The baby in the car	Throws the child in the trunk.

10 Signs
You've Turned

INTO YOUR
FATHER

1. When you walk around the house annoyed that all the lights are on.

2. When you eat leftovers from your child's plate over the trash can because "it would be a shame to throw food away."

3. When you fall asleep at 9:30pm in front of the TV.

4. When you yell at kids who are playing in the street to "Be quiet! There's a sleeping baby here!!!"

5. When you tell your child that "Money doesn't grow on trees!"

6. When you approach a puddle, you pick your little one up and say, "Careful!" instead of jumping in.

7. When you keep a folding chair and a beach umbrella in the trunk of your car.

8. When you have your own tool kit.

9. When you calculate how much you've spent on the child until now and how much he'll owe you when he leaves the house.

10. When your partner says, "You sound just like your father."

- the -
STATISTICS!

 **90%** of being a dad is developing an automatic side-eye in response to "Daddy, look at me!"

 **90%** of being a dad is standing over your kids at the pool to give them shade.

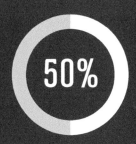 **50%** of the time you try to get the kids to play together.

 **50%** of the time you try to get the kids to stop fighting.

 **90%** of being a dad is getting home late from work, being upset that you don't have time with the kids, and swearing that tomorrow will be different. Every single day.

Note
to
Self

You realize just how little
you know about life
**only when your child
starts to ask you questions.**

CPSIA information can be obtained
at www.ICGtesting.com
Printed in the USA
LVHW072222051222
734659LV00011B/260